I Found a DEAD BIRD

The Kids' Guide to the Cycle of *Life & Death*

Jan Thornhill

MAPLE TREE PRESS

Maple Tree Press Inc.
51 Front Street East, Suite 200, Toronto, Ontario M5E 1B3
www.mapletreepress.com

Distributed in Canada by Raincoast Books
9050 Shaughnessy Street, Vancouver, British Columbia V6P 6E5

Distributed in the United States by Publishers Group West
1700 Fourth Street, Berkeley, California 94710

Cataloguing in Publication Data
Thornhill, Jan

I found a dead bird : the kids' guide to the cycle of life & death / Jan Thornhill.

ISBN-13: 978-1-897066-70-6 (bound) ISBN-10: 1-897066-70-8 (bound)
ISBN-13: 978-1-897066-71-3 (pbk.) ISBN-10: 1-897066-71-6 (pbk.)

1. Death—Juvenile literature. 2. Life cycles (Biology)—Juvenile literature.
I. Title.

HQ1073.3.T48 2006   j306.9   C2006-900750-0

Design: Jan Thornhill
Photography: see page 63

We acknowledge the financial support of the Canada Council for the Arts, the
Ontario Arts Council, the Government of Canada through the Book Publishing
Industry Development Program (BPIDP), and the Government of Ontario
through the Ontario Media Development Corporation's Book Initiative
for our publishing activities.

ONTARIO ARTS COUNCIL
CONSEIL DES ARTS DE L'ONTARIO

Printed in China

A   B   C   D   E   F

Contents

I Found a Dead Bird

It made me sad... **but**

I also had a lot
of questions, like:
Why did it have to die?
How did it die?
What would happen to it
now that it was

DEAD?

In this book, we're going to try to answer
questions like these, and LOTS MORE...

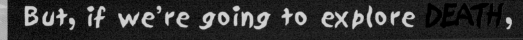
But, if we're going to explore **DEATH**,

first we have to answer some questions about

LIFE

What does it mean to be alive?

Why are some lives long?

Why are some lives short?

Do all living things eventually die?

It's a Fact of Life:
Everything That Lives Will One Day Die

For many of us, talking about death, or even thinking about it, is **scary**. This is partly because we worry about losing people we love, which is understandable. But **avoiding** the topic of death can add to our fears.

Death Is All Around Us

Though the idea of death can make us uncomfortable, we are surrounded by it. We eat meat and vegetables that were once living animals and plants. We squash insects when we walk outside. And, even now, special cells are destroying unfriendly bacteria inside our bodies. Everywhere on earth, living things are dying — but, at the same time, many more lives are just beginning.

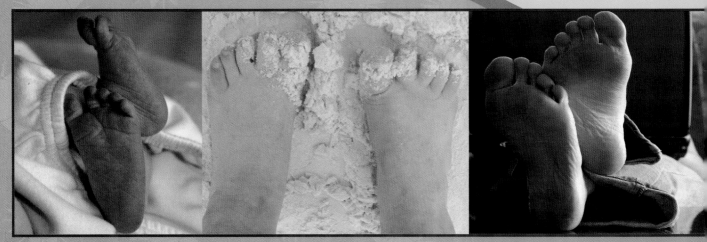

Each and every living thing on earth has a **beginning** to its life and an **end**.

Single-celled organisms begin life when one cell splits into two separate cells. Plants produce seeds that germinate and grow into new plants. Humans, like most other mammals, begin their lives inside a mother's uterus.

Sometimes lives last for only a few hours, other times for many, many years. But, short or long, every life will eventually end. We call this ending of a life **death**.

But **life** on earth goes on. After a living thing dies, its remains decompose and are gradually broken down into molecules, the building blocks of all living things. New lives spring up from the old.

This ongoing pattern is called the **cycle of life**.

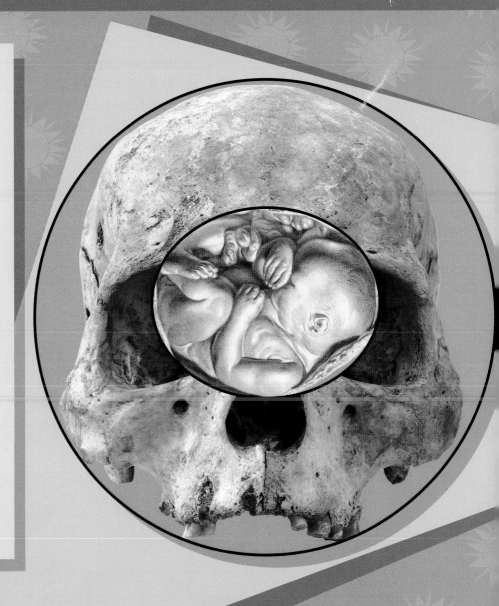

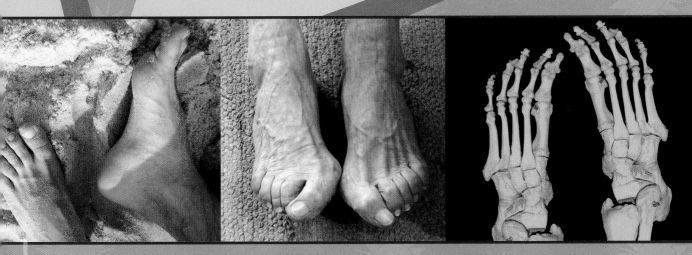

What Is LIFE?

Life is a process. It's what happens to **living things** between the moment their lives begin and the moment they die.

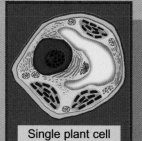
Single plant cell

So, What Is a Living Thing?

All living things:

- are made up of cells

- take in energy and get rid of waste

- grow and develop

- make copies of themselves

- react to their surroundings

A frog eats a baby cayman.

Growth rings of a spruce tree

A cat reacts to a fly.

Mother and daughter look-alikes

Teeming with Life...

Scientists think we share the earth with up to 30 million different kinds of living things, or **species**. Some species, like moose and daffodils, are easy to see. Others can only be seen under a microscope.

Almost all the bigger species — the mammals, the birds, the trees — have been found and named. But all over the planet there are still thousands of insects and fungi, and millions of micro-organisms, still waiting to be discovered!

Numbers of Named Species
(Approximate)

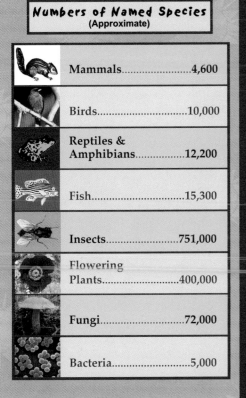

Mammals	4,600
Birds	10,000
Reptiles & Amphibians	12,200
Fish	15,300
Insects	751,000
Flowering Plants	400,000
Fungi	72,000
Bacteria	5,000

Species Populations
(Estimates)

Humans in the World	6,500,000,000
Dogs in the World	500,000,000
Blue whales in the World	1,600
Pandas in the World	1,000
Bald eagles in North America	100,000
Rats in New York City	70,000,000
Raccoons in Toronto	750,000
Bacteria in the Human Body	1 quadrillion

That's a LOT of LIFE!

So what would happen if there was no death?

WHAT IF

FLIES DIDN'T DIE?

If all the offspring of a single housefly survived to multiply, and all *their* young survived, and so on and so on, in only four months an area the size of the Amazon rain forest would be covered waist-deep in flies.

YUCK!

All Lives Have a Middle

All lives have a beginning, a middle, and an end. We call the middle the **lifespan**. For some species, a normal lifespan is very short — many bacteria live only an hour or two — while for others it can be very long. The average lifespan of a giant sequoia tree is more than 2,000 years, and some are more than 3,500 years old!

The largest living things in the world are giant sequoias. Some are so big you could build 45 family homes from a single tree.

A Billion Heartbeats

Tiny mammals have much shorter lives than bigger mammals. But big or small, mammals' hearts all end up beating about the same number of times during their lifespans — **one billion**. This works out because smaller hearts beat much faster than big ones. Humans are one of the few exceptions to this rule. Our hearts beat about 60 times a minute, which means we should live only 30 years — and that's exactly how long primitive man used to live thousands of years ago. But because of better nutrition and living conditions our hearts average **3 billion beats** in a lifetime!

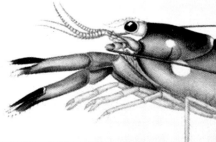

When humans age, their hair turns gray, they get wrinkles, they move more slowly. But a number of other living things, such as sea urchins, turtles, lobsters (above), and many fish, show no signs of aging — they just get bigger. The **biggest lobster** ever caught was 100 years old and weighed as much as a five-year-old child! But since lobsters don't die of old age, there might be even bigger granddaddies than that hiding deep in the ocean today.

30 beats/min.   60 beats/min.   600 beats/min.

Life Expectancy

Life expectancy is the most likely length of time that a plant or animal will live if all goes well. But just because an organism *can* live a long time, doesn't mean it *will* live a long time.

Life expectancy for a **mouse** is about three years, and many pampered pet mice will live this long. But a wild mouse that has to find food and avoid predators will probably live only a few weeks.

Life Expectancies
(and Known Records)

Elephant	70–80 yrs. (89)		Alligator	40–50 yrs. (66)
Black bear	15–20 yrs. (30)		Goldfish	5–10 yrs. (43)
Dog	10–12 yrs. (24)		Starfish	4–6 yrs. (20)
Beaver	10–15 yrs. (23)		Ant (Queen)	3 yrs. (15) Worker 2 wks.–6 months
Squirrel	8–9 yrs. (15)		Earthworm	4–15 yrs. (15)
Hummingbird	3–6 yrs. (9)		Maple tree	300–400 yrs. (500)
Goose	10–20 yrs. (20)		Lichen	1,000–4,000 yrs.
Copperhead snake	7 yrs. (30)		Bacteria	20 min.–250 million yrs.

Thanks to better living conditions, the average human life is longer now than ever before. But there is still a huge difference in life expectancy between **rich** and **poor** countries.

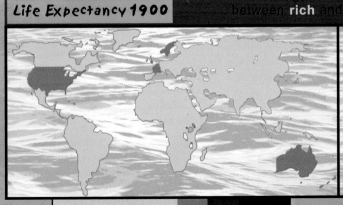

Life Expectancy 1900

Average lifespan (yrs.)   45 55 65 75

Life Expectancy 2000

Average lifespan (yrs.)   45 55 65 75

Some Lives Are Extraordinarily LONG

All living things have an **expected lifespan**. But one species might outlive another or, sometimes, an individual will live an unexpectedly long time. A tree might survive forest fires and droughts, or a person might be just plain lucky — and suddenly a record is set.

Insects

Insects generally live short lives, often only a few days. But there are exceptions. The longest-lived insect is the periodical cicada. Its long life begins when a nymph emerges from an egg. The nymph tunnels underground where it sucks juices from tree roots. **Seventeen years** later, it digs its way out to find a mate.

This adult cicada that has just emerged from its nymph shell will die within 6–8 weeks.

Land Animals

The giant tortoises are the longest-lived land animals with an average lifespan of 100 years. The oldest living Galapagos tortoise turned **176** in 2006, but scientists see no reason why it won't live to be at least **200**.

HUMANS Win the Mammal Prize!

The oldest human being was Jeanne Calment from France, who died in 1997 at the age of **122**. She drank two glasses of port every day, loved sweets, and rode a bicycle until she was a hundred! More people than ever are seeing their 100th birthday, making them **centenarians**.

Erma Louise Fox ("Foxy") celebrated her 100th birthday by going for a ride in a hot-air balloon and trying out a new water sport (left).

Under the Sea

The oldest fish ever found was a **205-year-old** rougheye rockfish. Scientists can figure out the age of fish by thinly slicing oddly shaped ear bones and counting growth rings. These ear bones are called otoliths.

Otolith of an 11-year-old flounder

Oldest Animal

It's not very big or showy, but the proven record holder for oldest animal on earth is a **220-year-old** ocean quahog clam (right) — aged by counting the growth rings on its shell. But scientists think that two other sea creatures probably grow even older — the red sea urchin, and a type of tubeworm found in the Gulf of Mexico.

But the PRIZE for longest life goes to...

...well, it seems that nobody really knows for sure what should win. Maybe it's "Methuselah," a bristlecone pine tree like the one shown here. "Methuselah" is almost 4,800 years old, older even than the Egyptian pyramids. Or maybe it's an exciting creosote bush in the Mojave Desert in the American Southwest. One circle of these shrubs has been growing outwards for possibly **12,000** years. The only problem is — the oldest part, the center, rotted out and disappeared thousands of years ago. So, does that count?

But maybe it's a lower form of life. Recently, scientists have been able to grow bacteria from **250-million-year-old** spores found in salt crystals buried deep in a cave in New Mexico!

Some Lives Are Very SHORT

LOOK OUT LITTLE GUYS!

For most living things, the beginning of life is a very **dangerous** time. Eggs are eaten or fail to hatch, seeds land in unfriendly places, or are eaten as soon as they sprout. And many mammals and birds are born so helpless they fall easy prey to predators.

Turtle eggs are often dug up and eaten by skunks or raccoons before they have a chance to hatch.

Predators find it easier to separate newborn herd animals from the crowd than adults. The wolf and coyote in the background already have a carcass, so these two elk calves are safe for the moment.

Sometimes human babies are born too early. With modern medical help many, like this one, will survive. But others are just too small and weak to make it.

Seeds and Spores

Most plants produce many more seeds than will ever sprout. Seeds often have very specific needs, and each species' needs are different. Many need the temperature to be just right before they can germinate. Others must have a particular amount of moisture. Some seeds are so specialized they have to pass through an animal's digestive system before they can sprout!

Think about the bread you eat. An average loaf is made from about 10,000 grains of wheat — that's 10,000 seeds that will never grow into plants!

Fungi reproduce by releasing huge numbers of minute spores. A single giant puffball, like this one, can produce **seven trillion** spores — that's enough to circle the earth's equator! But even though the puffball produces so many spores, almost none will find the perfect conditions to grow.

A Life and Death Experiment

To see how hard it is for young plants to survive, plant five dried beans in soil, one per section of an egg carton. Keep them moist and warm. After they have sprouted and grown several leaves, separate the sections. See what happens over time when you do the following:

Put one in a sunny warm window and keep it moist.	Put one in a sunny warm window and keep it very, very wet.	Put one in a sunny warm window and let the soil dry completely.	Put one in a warm, dark closet and keep it moist.	Put one in the refrigerator and keep it moist.

How Things DIE

There are many ways that living things die.

Think about a common

FLY

How many ways can you think of that a fly might die?

Drowning

Being swatted

Being shmushed

And, of course, being

EATEN

EVERYBODY Has to EAT

Everything alive must **consume energy** to survive, from the most minute microbe to the tallest tree, from the teensiest worm to the biggest whale.

What's for Supper?

Living things take in **energy** in different ways. Green plants capture energy from the sun and change it into sugars. Bacteria and other tiny microbes absorb food through their cell walls. Jellyfish trap tiny sea creatures with their stinging tentacles, which then drag the food directly into their stomachs. And, of course, many animals, from sharks to hummingbirds to humans, get energy by taking food into their bodies through their mouths.

Plants

Green plants make their own food by using chlorophyll to capture the sun's energy. When this energy is combined with water and carbon dioxide, sugar is produced.

Fungi

Fungi live inside their food, breaking it down with enzymes and absorbing nutrients with threadlike filaments called hyphae which mat together into mycelium.

Microbes

Tiny microbes absorb food from the outside in. This protozoan gradually changes shape to engulf its dinner, a paramecium.

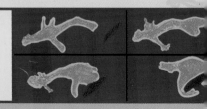

Who Eats What?

All living things are consumers. And, in turn, all living things are eventually consumed by other living things.

PLANTS consume energy from the sun.

HERBIVORES eat plants.

CARNIVORES eat animals.

OMNIVORES eat pretty much anything.

PARASITES eat living plants and animals.

SCAVENGERS eat the dead.

In an **ocean food chain**, microscopic plantlike phytoplankton are eaten by tiny animals called zooplankton. The zooplankton are eaten by sardine, the sardine by herring. The seal eats the herring and then the shark eats the seal. Who do you think eats the shark?

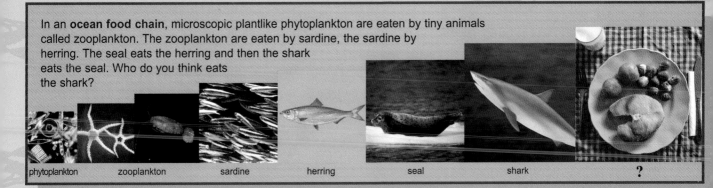

| phytoplankton | zooplankton | sardine | herring | seal | shark | ? |

Criss-Crossing Food Chains Make Food Webs

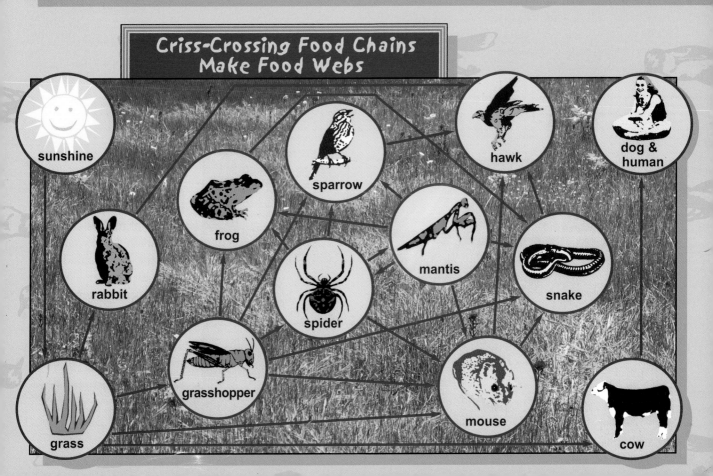

sunshine, sparrow, hawk, dog & human, frog, rabbit, mantis, snake, spider, grasshopper, mouse, grass, cow

Hungry HERBIVORES

Almost all life on earth depends on energy that comes from the sun. Green plants are the only life forms that can capture the **sun's energy** and turn it into food for other living things.

In the web of life, plants are **PRIMARY PRODUCERS**. Herbivores — living things that eat plants — are **PRIMARY CONSUMERS**, and, wow, can herbivores ever consume!

Tent Caterpillars

Tent caterpillars, the larvae of moths, are so plentiful in some years that in only a few weeks they can eat almost every leaf in a forest. Most trees will produce a second set of leaves later in the season, so the forest is not seriously harmed.

Busy Beavers

When beavers cut down trees, they eat the green bark and tender leaves, then use the branches to build lodges and dams. Their dams can flood vast areas of woodland, killing even more trees. But eventually the ponds fill in with silt and become meadows, providing grassy food for other herbivores.

Locusts

Locusts have voracious appetites for vegetation. Sometimes they gather in swarms of millions that can darken the sky and leave the earth behind as barren as a desert. The largest locust swarms can easily consume 10,000 tons of vegetation a day, and are particularly fond of farmers' crops.

Underwater Grazers

Most of the herbivores in the world's oceans feed on tiny green phytoplankton. But there are other vegetarians, too, that eat bigger underwater plants. The sea urchin is one of these creatures. Its favorite food is kelp (above), a type of seaweed. When there are too many sea urchins, they can cause great damage to the ancient kelp forests that protect young fish and other sea creatures. This happens when the number of urchin predators, such as sea otters, falls.

Red and purple sea urchins

How a Cow Chows

Cows and other grass grazers have a special stomach, called a rumen, where hard-to-digest plant matter is broken down into absorbable nutrients. Billions of tiny bacteria and protozoa help in this process. So, while a cow grazes in a meadow, a huge colony of miniature herbivores — too small to see — is happily grazing away in the cow's rumen.

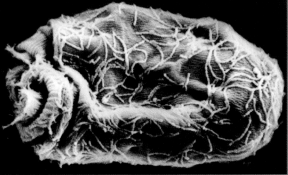

(Above) An electron micrograph shows a greatly magnified protozoan, covered with smaller rod-shaped bacteria, that was found in a cow's rumen.

Where's the MEAT?

Some living things eat animals. A number of these meat-eaters are **scavengers** that eat the remains of dead animals, but many are **predators**. Predators actively hunt other animals and kill them, often with the help of specialized skills or body parts.

A great grey owl's keen eyesight and hearing, along with powerful beak and talons, make it a formidable predator of small mammals.

Bloodthirsty Plants

Carnivorous plants attract, capture, and eat animals — usually insects. Some, like the pitcher plant (left), have downward pointing hairs inside cup-shaped leaves that prevent insects from crawling out. Others, like the Venus flytrap, have spiky leaf lobes that snap shut around their victims. Sundews have multiple tentacles on their leaves covered with attractive nectar and a sticky glue. Digestive enzymes turn bugs into protein soup that the plants can then absorb.

Wolves in Ants' Clothing

Have you ever been stung by an ant? Imagine being attacked by a pack of 50,000! That's what small creatures in South America have to worry about when army ants are on the move. There can be **2 million** of these tiny carnivores in a single colony, marching in a wide column across the forest floor. A swarm will attack whatever insects or lizards or spiders they come across, grasping them with their hooked jaws — called mandibles — and stinging them.

Because the army ant's sting is painful, people have to leave their homes for an hour or so when a swarm is passing through. But some don't find this an inconvenience since the ants will rid their households of other insect pests!

Close-up of an army ant showing its hooked mandibles

22

Killers of the Sea

With hundreds of razor-sharp teeth set in powerful jaws, and an incredibly acute sense of smell, sharks are the ocean's top predators. But what really gives them an edge is an extra sense called **electroreception**, which allows them to pick up incredibly tiny electrical signals. Since fish — and humans, too — all produce small amounts of electrical energy, a shark's electroreceptors can help it find well-hidden prey, even in the dark.

Should we worry about shark attacks when we're swimming in the ocean?

Look at it this way: Worldwide there are about 50 shark attacks on humans every year, resulting in 4–5 deaths. Humans, on the other hand, kill 30–100 million sharks a year. Maybe it's the sharks that have to worry.

Doesn't it Hurt to be Killed?

The instant an animal senses a threat to its life, its central nervous system triggers the release of special chemicals that act like rocket fuel for the body. Some of these chemicals speed up the heart and breathing and release stored energy to help the animal escape. Other chemicals dull pain.

Pain is a natural defense. If you touch a toasted marshmallow that's too hot, pain will make you pull your fingers away. But too much pain is not useful for an animal caught by a predator. It might distract it from its main task — getting away. So the prey animal's body sometimes produces strong painkillers, painkillers that also make the end more bearable if the animal can't escape.

World's #1 Predator

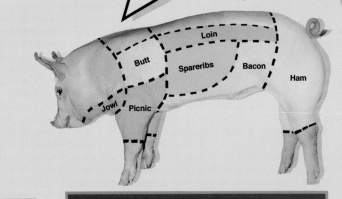

Loin

Butt

Spareribs

Bacon

Ham

Jowl

Picnic

No – it's not the pig. It's us!

Humans started out as hunters and gatherers. We hunted animals and we gathered plants. Time passed and we managed to tame many of the animals we liked to eat. We tended them and fed them, and when we were hungry for a T-bone steak or a chicken drumstick, we ate them. And we still do.

Our species' taste for meat has not gone away. Around the world we kill more than a billion pigs for pork every year and 300 million cattle for beef.

Lioness and Cape buffalo

Wild Weather

Weather is the **state of the atmosphere** outside. It can be hot and windy, or foggy and damp, or snowy and cold — or any other combination of these things. Mostly we don't worry about it much. We put on rubber boots or sunscreen or winter clothes and go about our business. Sometimes, though, when conditions are just right, weather can turn deadly.

ZAP!

This tree survived a lightning strike, but the huge gash down its trunk is an open invitation to insects and disease. →

Fire!

Lightning alone is not a huge killer, but forest fires started by lightning strikes can result in massive loss of life. Though most animals escape the flames by hiding in burrows or running or flying away, plant life is not so mobile. But, surprisingly, these fires are necessary for the long-term health of many of the world's forests. Ash adds nutrients to the soil, and leafless trees open up the ground to sunlight, allowing a new generation of trees to grow. Some tree seeds actually need a wildfire to sprout!

Two elk find refuge in a river from the flames of a forest fire.

Tornadoes and hurricanes are some of the most deadly forces of nature. Hurricanes, which form over warm oceans, are so huge they can easily be seen from space. Tornado funnels, though smaller, can pack such a punch they've been known to drive slivers of wood into iron fire hydrants!

The swirling winds of a strong tornado can be twice as fast as the winds of the worst hurricane and are devastating where they touch down. But the destruction caused by hurricanes when they hit land is always much more widespread.

Rain – Too Much, Too Little

Sometimes weather can kill without being outwardly violent. A lack of rain for a long time, or drought, can cause widespread death. Plants shrivel and die. Creek beds dry up, stranding fish and other aquatic animals. Famine occurs when drought causes crops to fail and large numbers of people go hungry.

Too much rain can be just as bad as too little. Rivers can overflow their banks, causing floods that drown crops and animals, and sometimes people, too. Every time it rains there are small-scale floods. Have you ever seen a dead earthworm in a puddle after a rain? That was a death by flood!

Tiny but Deadly

Infectious diseases are illnesses that can spread from one individual to another. Many can be fatal. Caused by microscopic organisms, they can strike almost any form of life, anywhere on the planet.

Even bacteria get deadly viruses!

Spore of fungus

Actual Size =

Elm bark beetle

Plant Diseases

Plants fall victim to all kinds of diseases caused by fungi, bacteria or viruses. Most of these diseases, like Dutch elm disease, can spread easily from plant to plant. Dutch elm disease was named for where it was first identified. Many other plant diseases are named for symptoms seen when a plant is sick, names like leaf curl, charcoal rot, rust, wilt, and frogeye leaf spot.

What would you name a disease that looked like this?

Millions of elms have been killed by Dutch elm disease, a fungus spread by tiny bark beetles.

Human Diseases

Infectious disease is responsible for millions of human deaths each year. Lucky for us, where many of us live, modern medicine and good living conditions help to keep us healthy. In some parts of the world, though, life is not so easy and thousands of children die every day from infectious diseases. The biggest killers are diarrhea caused by bacteria that breed in dirty water, malaria spread by mosquitoes, AIDS, and even measles. Solving the problem of poverty in these parts of the world would go a long way to stopping the spread of these diseases.

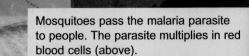
Mosquitoes pass the malaria parasite to people. The parasite multiplies in red blood cells (above).

Accidental Death

Once in a while a beaver will be killed by a falling tree or an ant will be stepped on by an elephant. But for many animals, including humans, most deadly accidents have something to do with people.

Human Accidents

(approx. number of North American deaths per year)

Car accidents — 22,000

Furniture falls — 860

Plane crashes — 710

Road Kill

In North America, roads and highways cross through every imaginable habitat — and on those roads we drive cars and trucks. Inevitably, our vehicles strike and kill animals. A lot of animals. It's estimated that almost a million birds, mammals, reptiles, and amphibians are killed every day on our roads and highways.

Electrocution — 475

Bathtub drowning — 400

Poison liquids — 120

Fireworks — 7

Snake bites — 4

Vending machines — 2

Window Collisions

Birds fly — and they're good at it. They easily avoid crashing into trees and mountainsides. Unfortunately, they haven't yet learned to recognize window glass. It's estimated that every year at least a hundred million birds die from collisions with window glass — and that's only in North America!

You Can Help!

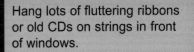

Hang lots of fluttering ribbons or old CDs on strings in front of windows.

Close your curtains during the day, especially during the spring and fall migration season.

If you enjoy feeding birds, the feeders should be placed either very close to windows (½ m or 1½ ft.) or far away (at least 10 m or 10 yds.).

These are only a few of the hummingbirds found dead near office towers in Toronto by rescue volunteers during one migration season.

27

Human Destruction

Every person on the planet needs to eat and needs a place to live. But there are more than half a billion of us on the planet.

6,500,000,000 people need:

- a lot of food
- a lot of water
- a lot of space
- a lot of fuel
- a lot of everything

And that spells trouble for other living things.

Taking Too Much

People have been killing animals for food and to protect their crops forever. The farm families above pose behind the results of a "jackrabbit drive" in the 1890s. These drives were organized in the American West to deal with an exploding rabbit population that did great damage to crops. Jackrabbits have survived, but other animals have not fared so well. We have hunted species, such as the dodo, into extinction, and fish stocks all over the world are now drastically low from overfishing.

What a Mess!

Humans pollute by releasing harmful waste into the environment. We dump garbage, we spew gases from cars and factories, we spill dangerous chemicals and oil. Many of these pollutants are not just unhealthy — they're deadly, and they're showing up everywhere on earth.

Thousands of marine animals, including seals, suffer from oil spills in the world's oceans. Oil is being cleaned off the pups on the right with an absorbent material.

There Goes the Neighborhood

An area of clear-cut forest

Many of the world's plants and animals are in trouble due to habitat loss. Humans clear-cut forests for wood, and to make way for agriculture and cities and towns. We drain wetlands, build dams and change the way rivers flow. This leaves less space for the animals and plants that have always lived in these places. As a result, many species are in danger of extinction solely because of the way humans have altered their habitats. We even do it in smaller ways — every time you wash your hands, the soap you use makes the environment for bacteria unlivable!

When People Kill People

One of the half-million casualties of the American Civil War (1861–1865)

It isn't only other species that have to worry about people. People have to worry about people, too. We have a very bad habit of killing each other. Sometimes it's one person murdering another. Other times, though, we wage war, and that's when incredible numbers of lives are lost. In the twentieth century alone more than **200 million** people died as a direct result of wars.

Death of a Species

When every member of a **species** dies, the species is extinct.
Gone forever.
Kaput.

R. I. P.

Saber-tooth tiger
10,000 BC

Giant beaver
8,000 BC

Dodo
1681

Passenger pigeon
1914

These are just a few of the species that have become extinct since humans have been around. The giant beaver, three times the size of today's beavers, and the saber-tooth cats disappeared near the end of the last ice age. The passenger pigeon, once so plentiful that flocks blackened the sky, was hunted to extinction. The blue pike was overcome in its natural lake habitat by foreign, introduced species.

But these are just a drop in the bucket — it's estimated that almost **a third** of the world's species are in danger of going extinct before the year 2100.

Xerces blue
1941

Labrador duck
1878

Blue pike
1983

Carolina parakeet
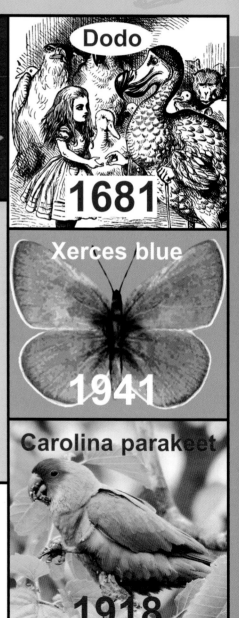
1918

Mass Extinction

Most mass extinctions, like the one that killed off the dinosaurs, have been due to climate change caused by giant meteor impacts or extreme volcanic activity. But one very early extinction event was different: it was caused by a living thing — cyanobacteria.

Cyanobacteria was the first life form to produce oxygen as a waste product, like plants do today. As time passed, though, the huge colonies of cyanobacteria spewed out so much oxygen that other life forms were poisoned and went extinct. But this is what created the oxygen-rich atmosphere that almost all life on earth depends on today.

Scientists say that between 1 and 100 species are being lost around the world every day, mostly because of habitat destruction. Will human beings be the second form of life to cause a mass extinction?

Cyanobacteria still exists today.

The manatee is only one of thousands of species at risk of extinction today.

Mass Extinction: a catastrophic loss of many species in a short time

SMALLPOX:
Erasing a Species on Purpose

Smallpox virus

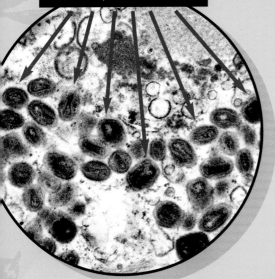

Hundreds of millions of people have been killed by the smallpox virus — so it's little wonder that we've tried to get rid of it. The fall of smallpox began when it was noticed that people who survived a bout with the disease were immune to it for the rest of their lives. The search for a vaccine began. Almost a thousand years ago, smallpox scabs were ground up into a powder that was blown up the nostrils of people who had never had smallpox. Some of these people developed a milder form of the disease and didn't die. But it wasn't until the twentieth century that a truly effective vaccine was developed. Use of this vaccine was so successful that in May, 1980, the world was declared free of smallpox.

People with smallpox develop a high fever and a bumpy rash.

BUT

...smallpox is not quite extinct. A small amount of the virus still exists in a few laboratories for research purposes.

So, what happens After something dies?

At almost the exact moment **a living thing dies**, its remains begin to break down and decay.

BUT that's not all!

Decay: to decompose, and become soft, crumbly, or liquefied

...Things can get pretty lively around the dead!

A crow will eat a dead rat...

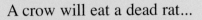

...and so will a skunk...

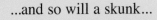

...and so will a carrion beetle...

...and so will a wasp...

...and so will fly maggots...

...and so will bacteria...

Bit by bit, by being gnawed at by teeth or the mouthparts of insects, by being digested by fungi, by being dissolved by enzymes, or by being liquefied by bacteria, every dead thing is eventually broken down into the building blocks of all **new life**.

...and so will all kinds of other things...

The Moment of DEATH

Death: the end of all life processes of an organism as a whole

The most obvious outward sign of death in a mammal, bird, or fish is that the animal stops breathing. The eyes may or may not close. The heart stops beating. Starved of oxygen, brain cells immediately begin to die. When enough brain cells have died, the point of no return has been reached.

A Changing Definition

People used to rely solely on a lack of breath and pulse to pronounce someone dead. But we have learned that a stopped heart can sometimes be started again. Most people now agree that the moment of death is when all parts of the brain, particularly the brainstem, cease functioning.

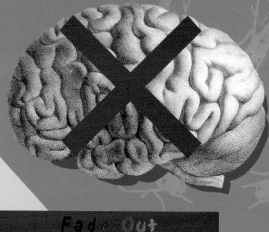

Fade Out

The beautiful colors of fish are made by special cells in their skin called **chromatophores**. These cells allow fish to change color in response to their environment. Some fish change color when they're ready to spawn, like the sockeye salmon shown here, or if they are stressed. When a fish is caught and pulled from the water, the life-and-death stress of the situation instantly causes its brighter colors to fade. So a fish out of water will never look quite the same as a healthy fish swimming underwater.

Living sockeye salmon

Dead sockeye salmon

Stiff as a Board

Immediately after an animal dies, its muscles relax and go completely limp. Over the next few hours, a chemical reaction caused by oxygen starvation inside the muscles makes them seize up and become stiff. This freezing of the muscles is called **rigor mortis**. Rigor mortis lasts for a day or two, and then the muscles relax again. Another change is called **liver mortis**. When blood is no longer being pumped through the body by the heart, gravity makes it accumulate in those parts lying closest to the ground. This pooling causes "lividity" — discoloration of the skin, like big bruises.

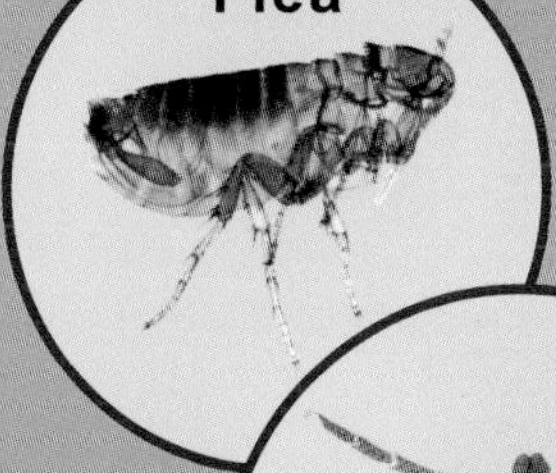

Flea

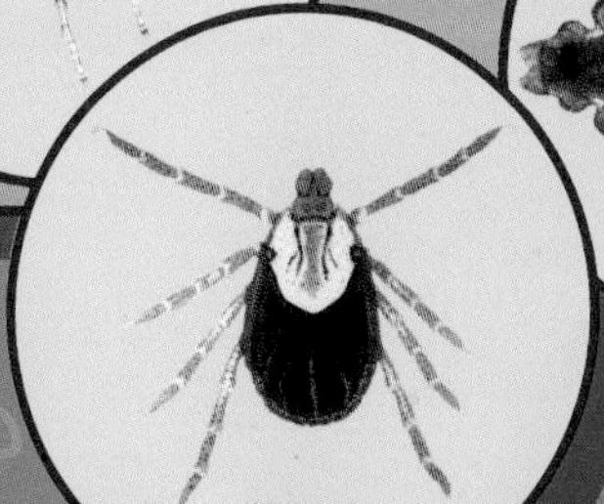

Mite

Tick

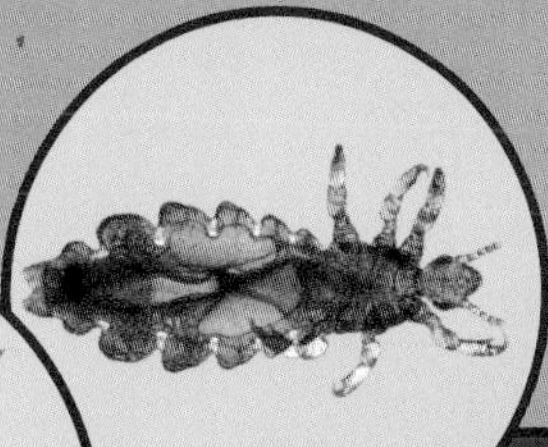

Louse

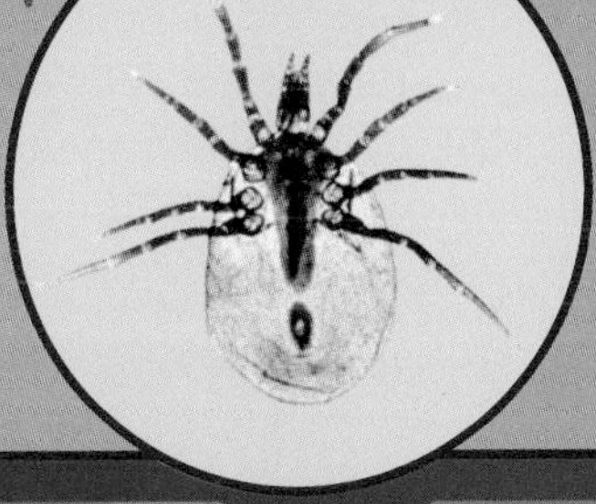

See Ya Later!

When an animal, like the young robin shown here, dies, its blood stops flowing. Blood-sucking parasites sense this immediately. Without the fresh blood they need to survive, they leave the corpse in droves to search out a new, living host. This is one of the reasons why you should always wear gloves if you have to move a dead animal. Better yet, use a shovel.

Scavengers

Scavengers eat **already dead** plant and animal matter. They're the garbage collectors of the world. Without scavengers cleaning up the dead, our planet would be a really stinky, messy place.

Coyotes, like this one on an elk carcass, are frequent scavengers. Coyotes are protected from food poisoning by a special receptor in the brain, which makes them immediately throw up anything that is dangerously rotten.

Mini Clean-up Crew

Specialized white blood cells called **macrophages** are the human body's live-in scavengers. They scour every nook and cranny looking for bacteria and dead or damaged cells to eat. They can also detect viruses and other foreign matter — when they do, they help trigger an immune response. Scientists are hoping to use macrophages to fight diseases and cancer.

Magnified 7,000 times!

A macrophage reaches out for debris to eat.

Dedicated Scavengers

Vultures only eat carrion — the meat of dead animals — and they're perfect for the job. They have a well-developed sense of smell. Their heads are often bald to reduce the amount of rotting matter sticking to them. Strong acids in their digestive systems destroy harmful bacteria. Their urine is also very acidic, so they pee down their legs to kill nasty bacteria that clings to them.

A turkey vulture suns itself, both to warm up and to help kill off bacteria picked up from dead animals.

Hermit crabs not only eat decaying matter, they live inside the shells of dead mollusks.

In the Sea

The world's oceans are packed with scavengers. Most eat "sea snow," tiny plant and animal particles that drift down from above. When a large animal, such as a whale, dies, it sinks to the bottom where it provides an ongoing feast for a multitude of scavengers. Crustaceans, small fish, and sharks pick away at the carcass. Slimy, eel-like hagfish burrow inside and eat their way out. Later, tiny snails and other mollusks feed on dissolving nutrients. Bacteria, mussels, clams, and crabs gradually ingest the bones. Fifteen years later, the whale carcass is gone.

Stinky Tricksters

Many scavengers use their sense of smell to find a meal. Even vultures rely on scent to find rotting meat, and many insects do, too. Some plants and fungi take advantage of this attraction to the smell of death. One is the aptly named stinkhorn (left). Instead of relying on air to send its reproductive spores far and wide like other fungi, the stinkhorn produces its spores in a slimy, smelly mass. Scavenger insects are drawn to the stink. When they discover there's nothing to eat, off they fly — but with the stinkhorn's spores now hitching a ride on their feet! A number of plants use the same ploy to help spread their pollen. The leafless rafflesia (right) not only smells bad, it also produces the largest flower in the world, a fleshy, polka-dotted blossom that can be as big as a hula hoop!

Decomposition of an Animal

Have you ever smelled food that's "gone bad"? Well, that's **decomposition** at work. And it can be pretty unpleasant.

The instant an animal dies its cells begin to dissolve from the inside out. Starved of oxygen, the cell walls weaken and fluid leaks out. After a few days the leaked fluid causes the skin of the corpse to blister and become loose. At the same time, all the billions of "good" bacteria that live inside an animal start gobbling up the dying cells. Bacteria release waste in the form of smelly gases. These gases escape the decomposing corpse in greater and greater amounts and attract scavengers of all sizes.

Humans think the smell of decay is awful, but vultures and other scavengers find the aroma powerfully attractive.

Lured by the tantalizing smell of death, flesh-eating flies arrive and lay eggs. Their larvae, or "maggots," set to work eating. Soon after, carrion beetles appear. Beetle larvae eat both fly maggots and flesh. Eventually so much flesh has been eaten and so much liquid has drained away that the corpse collapses. A new set of beetles with specialized mouthparts feast on the tough skin and ligaments that remain. Next come moths and bacteria that eat fur and feathers. When these various scavengers have done feeding, all that remains of the animal is its skeleton.

Blowflies, carrion beetles, and red-spotted burying beetles are just a few of the insects that feed on corpses.

Stage One (0–3 days)
- bacteria goes into action
- cell walls break down
- the first insects arrive

Stage Two (3–10 days)
- smelly gases are produced
- the corpse inflates
- more insects arrive

Stage Three (10–20 days)
- very strong smell
- liquids seep into ground
- skin bursts open

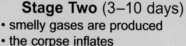

YUCK!

HOW GROSS!

Do some of these pictures revolt you? Does your face screw up in disgust when you smell a dead animal or rotting garbage? Well, guess what? Everybody in the world has exactly the same reaction. And everybody in the world has pretty much the same word for it, too — YUCK. If the smell of decomposition, or the sight of writhing maggots, didn't disgust us, we might eat food that's gone bad and then get sick from the bacteria that multiplies so rapidly on corpses.

So, go ahead and say it:

YUCK!

The head of a blowfly maggot magnified 70 times.

The bones of a deer

The Bones

Eventually all that is left of a corpse is the skeleton. Like other parts of the body, living bones have cells. But the bulk of bone matter is made up of minerals, like calcium. We drink milk or eat cheese to get calcium to make our own bones strong. Porcupines and mice and other rodents will gnaw on old bones for the same reason, which helps to break bones down. Weather and time do the rest, but it can take many years for a skeleton to disintegrate.

Stage Four (20–50 days)
- butyric acid causes cheesy smell
- mold grows
- beetles feed on tough parts

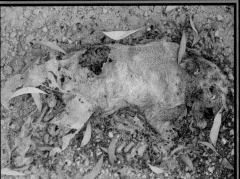

Stage Five (50–365 days)
- corpse dries
- decomposition slows
- moths and bacteria eat hair

Stage Six (1–100 years)
- corpse is reduced to skeleton
- animals gnaw on bones
- bones disintegrate into soil

Plant Decomposition

Dead plants, like animals, decompose in **stages**. For trees, the largest and most solid of plants, this process can take many years. While a dead tree is still standing, insects tunnel under its bark and into its woody core. Fungi and woodpeckers further weaken it until it falls to the forest floor. With the help of a multitude of organisms, the tree gradually breaks down into rich soil.

Ants and Termites

Colonies of carpenter ants (above) and some termites make their homes in dead wood. Termites eat wood wherever they find it — whether it's an old log or the walls of a house.

Unlike termites, carpenter ants don't actually eat the wood, but they help trees decompose by carving out intricate mazes of compartments (left) where they raise their young.

Beetles and Their Grubs

Many insect scavengers help decompose plants. The bessbug or "patent-leather beetle" (right) is a major forest decomposer. As it feeds on dead trees, it creates tunnels where it lays its eggs. The larvae, or grubs, eat the pre-chewed wood the adult leaves behind. Other beetles that prefer more decayed wood come later on.

Beetle larva

Gnawers and Clawers

Small animals, such as chipmunks (left), mice, shrews, and moles help to break down fallen logs by burrowing, while making spaces for their nests or searching for food. Bears and other larger animals will use their claws to tear apart decaying wood to get at juicy grubs.

Woodpeckers

Woodpeckers help break down dead or dying trees by prying off bark and pecking holes in trunks and limbs while searching for insects and their larvae. Woodpeckers have exceptionally long tongues that are covered with barbs or sticky saliva to help them extract insects from trees. Their strong beaks are also used to excavate nest holes in dead trees.

Creepy Things

Lift up any decaying matter in a forest and you are likely to find pill bugs and sow beetles or multi-legged centipedes and millipedes. These little invertebrates feed mostly on weather-softened dead plant matter, breaking it down into smaller pieces that attract minute wood mites.

Fungi

Fungi are major decomposers of wood and other plant matter. The various mushrooms and shelf fungi that you see growing on wood or on the ground are actually just the spore-producing parts of the organism, like the fruit of a plant. The main "body" of any fungus is its mycelium mat made up of threadlike hyphae that grow hidden beneath bark or underground. These parts excrete enzymes that "digest" even the hardest wood, softening it for other organisms to eat.

Earth to Earth

All living things return to the earth when they die. This process can be fast or slow, but it always happens and is absolutely necessary in the **cycle of life**.

Dirt Eaters

At night, earthworms stretch out of their burrows and drag plant debris back underground. They eat this debris along with generous helpings of soil particles to help with grinding. As the plant parts pass through the worm, they're broken down into essential soil nutrients that living plants need to grow.

Wood Grinders

Termites are one of the world's most important plant decomposers. They tunnel through wood, ingesting large amounts of cellulose. But most termites can't digest cellulose, and rely on protozoa and bacteria in their guts to break it down into nutrients they can use. Though termites look like white ants, and live in colonies like ants, they're actually more closely related to another important forest decomposer: the cockroach. Termites are only a problem when they invade buildings and cause structural damage.

Itsy Bitsy, Teeny Weeny

A single teaspoon of soil from almost anywhere in the world will contain between 100 million to 1 billion bacteria. Most of these bacteria are decomposers that convert tiny particles of organic matter into forms that are useful to other living things. Others convert nitrogen from the air into a form plants can use. Some even produce antibiotics! Soil that has no bacteria will not support higher life forms.

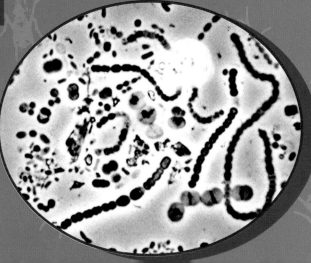

Micro-Menagerie

Forest soil is alive with an amazing variety of microscopic creatures, including minute arachnids called mites. An area the size of your foot might contain 50 or more different species of these spider relatives. They munch on all kinds of organic matter, producing tiny droppings that are in turn fed on by fungi and a wide variety of even smaller micro-organisms such as bacteria and protozoa.

Molds and Yeasts

Molds and yeasts are tiny fungi. Yeasts thrive on sugars. The holes you see in bread are made by the gases yeast cells expel as they eat. Molds, like the ones that appear on stale bread, grow like other fungi, as creeping mycelium mats. The mycelium spreads through organic matter and breaks it down with enzymes.

2-week-old bread

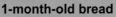

1-month-old bread

4-month-old bread

6-month-old bread

Sorry ...but we have to mention poop

LIFE-SIZE!

Most organic matter is eaten or in some way ingested by other living things. No matter what kind of digestive processes happen inside an animal, some form of waste is always produced. This waste is most noticeable when it comes from larger animals. We're talking poop. Excrement. Manure. Feces. Droppings. Guano. Scat. And just as we have a natural aversion to decomposition, we also like to steer clear of fecal matter, and for good reason. About one third of all excrement from any mammal is made up of bacteria. Some of this bacteria can make us sick. But most of it simply helps break down waste into nutrients for other life forms to use.

Moose scat shown here is made up of plant matter and bacteria.

TRAPPED in TIME

Part I

Sometimes, when conditions are just right, **decomposition doesn't happen** in the normal way — or doesn't happen at all.

Stuck

Amber is fossilized plant resin. Trees ooze resin to protect themselves from injury. Because resin is usually sticky, insects or other small vertebrates can get stuck in it. So sometimes amber holds perfectly preserved specimens of creatures that are millions of years old.

Mosquitoes trapped in amber

Dried

In very dry places — deserts or high in mountains — corpses can dehydrate, or mummify. This drying process can happen so quickly that bacteria and molds, which need moisture to survive, have little chance to cause decay. The skin and internal organs of the animal simply dry and harden. Long ago, ancient Egyptians buried their dead in the desert, producing natural mummies. Over the years, they made an art of mummification, using special techniques to dry out and preserve the dead before wrapping them in layers of cloth. Other cultures have also practiced mummification, using smoke or herbs to help preserve the bodies of their dead for thousands of years.

A naturally mummified lizard

This unwrapped Egyptian mummy must be kept in a tightly sealed case to prevent moisture from creeping in and triggering the process of decay.

Tanned

"Bog people" are human bodies that have been found in soggy peat bogs, where normal decay is slowed by natural acids and cold temperatures. Bacteria can't live in these oxygen-free conditions. Though the bones of the bog people have been eaten away by acidic water, the skin and inner organs are eerily well-preserved. Some stomachs even hold undigested bits of people's last meals! Archeologists think these people may have been killed and offered to the bogs as part of rituals or ceremonies, sometimes more than 2,000 years ago.

Though Tollund Man died more than 2,200 years ago, he is so well-preserved that the people who discovered him in 1950 thought they'd stumbled on a recent murder victim and called the police! Bog acids "tanned" his skin, making it dark and leathery.

Frozen

We put food in freezers to keep it from going bad. Nature preserves animals this way, too. A man, now called Otzi, complete with clothes, was found high in the Alps where he'd been frozen in ice for more than 5,000 years. We're learning amazing things from him about life in prehistoric times. Sometimes woolly mammoths and other extinct animals are found in the Far North that have been frozen since the last ice age. In most cases the animals had begun to decay before being frozen, but sometimes the remains are more intact. In one case, scientists made a stew of 36,000-year-old bison meat. They said it had a "strong Pleistocene aroma," but they ate it anyway!

Scientists have recently discovered several frozen woolly mammoths in Siberia. One had such well-preserved bone tissue that researchers have been able to map its genetic code. So far, they've found that its DNA is 98.5% identical to the DNA of African elephants. This means that some day it might be possible to combine genetic information from the two species and create an elephant-mammoth hybrid.

TRAPPED in TIME

Part II

Sometimes the remains of living things are preserved not just for thousands of years, but for **millions** of years. They're kept safe, locked in stone.

Fossilization

An animal dies and falls into water. Scavengers feed on its flesh and it begins to slowly decompose.	Sometimes, mud and sand are washed over the animal's remains and the hard parts, like bones and teeth, don't decay.	More and more layers of mud and sand cover the animal's remains. Years and years pass and these layers turn to rock.	Over millions of years, the bones and teeth are replaced with minerals. Fossilization is complete.

Stone Giants

Most people's favorite fossils are the big ones — dinosaur bones. The largest carnivore was not *T. rex* (right), but a similar meat-eater called *Giganotosaurus*. It was probably big enough to take on the largest dinosaur found to date — a long-necked herbivore called *Argentinosaurus*. Those guys were so big that a single fossilized vertebra, or back bone, dwarfs an average 11-year-old!

70 million years old!

Sea Creatures

Because fossils form in layers under water, it's only natural that we have found many remains of extinct sea creatures. And it's from this fossil record that we have learned so much about how life on earth evolved. For instance, we know that primitive sharks first appeared more than 400 million years ago.

Early Birds

Archaeopteryx (pronounced ar-kee-Op-ter-ix) is accepted as the earliest example we've found of a bird. But *Archaeopteryx* (right) was not very much like modern birds. Though it had feathers, it also had three claws on each wing, a long bony tail, and a full set of sharp teeth. Because some of these features are similar to those found in a few dinosaurs, many scientists think that *Archaeopteryx* is a powerful piece of evidence proving that birds evolved from dinosaurs.

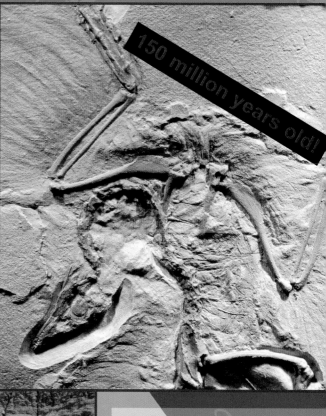

150 million years old!

225 million years old!

Plant Life

There are many examples of plant life that have been fossilized. Some of the most spectacular, and the biggest, are the trees found in the Petrified Forest in Arizona. These trees were buried under layers of volcanic ash, which eventually caused the cells of the trees to become fossilized with quartz crystals. Minerals combined with the quartz, making rainbows of colors.

When People Die

Sad but true:

Like all other living things, every human being will eventually die. But there's something that makes us different than other living things...

...we react to death

We cry over our dead

We respect our dead

We remember our dead

We question death

We learn from the dead

Grieving

Grieving, or **mourning**, when someone beloved dies is universal. People all over the world grieve. Even when there is a belief that the death of a body is not the death of a soul, people still feel sadness at the loss of someone close.

We show our sadness at losing a loved one in many ways. There are no right ways or wrong ways. Sometimes we cry. Sometimes we wail. Sometimes we have trouble sleeping or eating. Sometimes we talk to the person who has died. Sometimes we mourn by not showing our feelings at all. Almost always, though, we join together to share our sorrow.

Once in a while a catastrophe will take so many human lives that whole societies mourn. The massive tsunami of 2004 was one such event, as was the 9/11 tragedy. Because we hear so much about these things and see images of them on the news, they seem very close to us. Even if no one we know has died, we still feel sad. This is a special trait of humans — to be able to grieve for people we have never met.

A mourner at Ground Zero

Animals and Grief

Companion Animals

Often, the first experience we have with death is the loss of a pet. Many of us accept dogs and cats and other animals into our families, and we are capable of caring deeply for them. So when a pet dies, we grieve its loss. This works the other way, too — there are many stories of animals that seem to go into mourning when their human caregivers die.

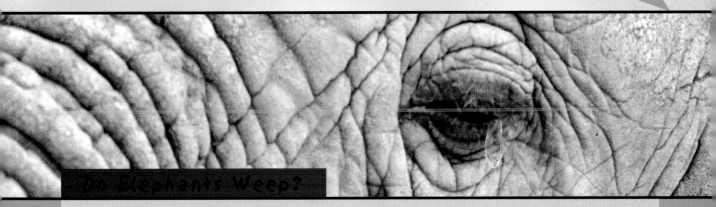

Do Elephants Weep?

Though many people think it isn't possible for animals to grieve over members of their own species, there is much evidence that they do. Female elephants have been known to stand over a dead calf for days, occasionally reaching out with their trunks to touch the corpse. Dolphins sometimes try to revive dead infants, and seals wail pitifully. A baby monkey or chimpanzee that has lost its mother might refuse to eat for so long that it starves to death. Even birds seem to mourn their own kind. Geese and parrots can be so devoted to their partners that when their mates die they show human signs of grief, becoming listless and droopy and refusing to eat.

Funeral Customs

Funeral customs are the things we do after a person dies. In most cultures, special ceremonies are held to **honor the dead**.

Wakes and Funerals

What happens at wakes and funerals depends on the beliefs of the deceased. Usually family and friends gather together. Sometimes the body of the dead person will be on view, which helps people accept the death. Sometimes a priest or other religious figure will perform special rites, or a family member will say some words. Often mourners are very solemn and quiet, but in some cultures people are expected to wail over their loss, or chant. Sometimes there is a procession. Many funerals end with the burial or cremation of the body.

Cemeteries

The earliest burials of primitive man were likely a way to protect the remains of the dead from scavengers. Later, ancient people "planted" the dead to ensure continued life. As communities grew, so did their burial places. City cemeteries — particularly in Europe — eventually became so over-crowded that the dead had to be stacked one on top of the other. This was such an unsanitary practice that in the 1800s many of these urban graveyards were closed and new, parklike ones were created outside of cities and towns.

Cremation

Cremation, or the burning of the remains of the dead, has been practiced for thousands of years. The ancient Romans cremated their dead and kept the ashes in decorative urns. Hindus prefer cremation to burial since they believe that ritual burning will free a person's spirit to move on into a new life. Many North Americans now choose to be cremated instead of being buried. Families often scatter the ashes in a place that was special to the deceased.

Many people keep the ashes of loved ones in special urns.

"Mourning" clothes are common in many cultures. In North America in the late 1800s, everyone wore black to funerals — and wore black for at least a year after a close relative's death.

A Multitude of Customs

A Chinese custom is to burn bundles of paper that represent money along with other paper objects to ensure that loved ones will have whatever they need in the afterlife. Paper items can be foods, like the fish above, or clothing or jewelry, or even modern conveniences such as radios and laptop computers.

All over the world different people have different customs and rituals associated with death. Sometimes a body must be washed a certain number of times, or covered in a colored cloth, or the feet must be pointing in a particular direction. Sometimes special words have to be whispered in a dead person's ear. Sometimes candles, or incense, or lanterns are lit. Sometimes special foods are eaten by mourners or are offered to the deceased.

Flowers have been a part of many funeral customs throughout history. Sometimes a body is covered with garlands, or flowers are sent to the family of the deceased, or placed on a grave. There is even evidence that Neanderthal man was buried with flowers 50,000 years ago!

53

Most people in the world agree on one thing — human beings have spirits or souls and, after death, these **spirits move on** to another existence.

The Soul Moves On

The soul moving on is not a new idea. Ancient humans buried their dead with food and other items, suggesting that they believed a person would still need such things in an afterlife. In modern religions, many people believe there is a "heaven," while others believe their spirits will return to earth in another form. But all major religions agree that the way a person lives his or her life determines what happens to the soul after physical death.

Once a year, in Mexico, during the celebration of *La Día de los Meurtos*, or the Day of the Dead, the spirits of loved ones are expected to drop by for a visit. Flowers, food, candy skulls, skeleton figures, and other items are arranged into altars to honor and welcome them.

Reincarnation

Hundreds of millions of people in the world believe that the lives they are now living are not their first, nor will they be the last. Some of these people — Hindus — believe that after the death of a body, the soul, or *atman*, will return, or be reincarnated into a new earthly form. They also believe that their actions during their lives decide what they will become in the next life. If they do good, they will reach a higher state of being; if they're bad, they could be reincarnated as a lower form of life.

Krishna, one of many incarnations of the Hindu god Vishnu, is always depicted with big eyes and blue skin.

Some people who have survived a life-threatening event, such as a heart attack, report an extraordinary experience when they are revived. Sometimes they say they looked down on their own bodies while medical teams worked on them. Some continue into a dark tunnel and move towards a light. Others report that they are greeted by dead relatives. Usually people have a sense of overwhelming peace. Many believe they have seen a glimpse of heaven. Scientists think these experiences might be an effect caused by brain cells starved of oxygen, which might briefly increase certain types of brain activity. But we still don't know for sure.

GHOSTS?!

Percentage of North Americans who believe in ghosts:

50%

Number of ghosts proven to exist:

0

Sightings of ghosts, and ghostly activities or "hauntings," have been recorded throughout history. The general belief is that ghosts are the spirits of deceased people that for some reason have remained on earth. But scientists now have several explanations for these strange reports. Surprisingly, the most promising one has to do with sound! Sound waves can sometimes get trapped in buildings, sound of such low frequency that the human ear can't hear it. But these sound waves can cause vibrations that not only make us feel chilled and uneasy, but actually make our eyeballs jiggle enough to blur parts of our vision, making us see "ghosts."

Memories

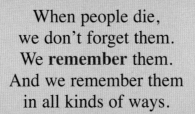

When people die,
we don't forget them.
We **remember** them.
And we remember them
in all kinds of ways.

Happy Times, Sad Times

Memories, more than anything else, are what make us feel connected to people long after they're gone. Sometimes, especially at first, these memories can be painful because they remind us of our loss. But as time passes, we come to cherish what we remember. Though memories can often be both happy and sad at the same time, or "bittersweet," they are a lasting gift given to us by those we have loved.

Mementos

People almost everywhere keep mementos to remind them of family members or friends who have died. We pass heirlooms down from one generation to the next, and we keep photo albums full of pictures. In the late 1800s, when having photographs taken was very expensive, often the only photos people had of family members were ones taken shortly after they had died, like this one of the little girl (left). A hundred years ago, it was common to fashion bracelets or wreaths out of hair cut from the deceased. Back then, many women carried small glass vials called "tear catchers." Whenever they wept with sorrow over a loved one who was gone, they would catch their tears in the bottle to keep as a memento.

Today, some people are having the carbon removed from the ashes of cremated loved ones and turned into diamonds.

Hair bracelet

Honoring Markers

For thousands of years, people all over the world have marked the final resting places of their dead as a way of both honoring and remembering them. The marker can be as simple as a rock-pile cairn or as complex and gigantic as the pyramids built by the ancient Egyptians for their pharaohs. Mostly, though, it's something in between. Stone markers are commonly used since they can last for centuries. In the Far North, wood, which decays slowly in cold climates, is often used. Sometimes the dead are placed under or inside structures, such as "spirit houses" or mausoleums.

(Counterclockwise from top) Cairn with flowers; Muslim cemetery; First Nations' spirit houses; stone cross; headstone, Scotland; angel decoration; tombstone, China; Jewish cemetery, Prague; mausoleum, Peru; pyramids, Egypt; desert grave, New Mexico; simple headstones

Species Memory

Everyone knows that a newborn's scream is astoundingly loud. But babies aren't taught to scream. They arrive in the world with the instinct, or "species memory," to make a lot of noise to get what they need. This and other human instincts — like the way we say "yuck" when we smell something rotten — have been passed down from one generation to the next for thousands of years. And each of us, in turn, will pass on these instincts to our own children. This not only helps to ensure the survival of our species, but will help to keep our great-great-great-great grandchildren safe and healthy many years after we, ourselves, are gone.

Learning from DEATH

The dead speak — not very loudly, but they can, and do, tell us a lot about ourselves, (and other species, too).

Looking Inside

For a long time, most societies had a taboo against cutting up the dead and peering inside. Humans, though, are curious animals. Scientists, doctors, and medical students slowly pushed for permission to dissect corpses. At first no one wanted to offer their departed loved ones for this purpose, so the corpses of criminals were used. Later, when it became clear that important medical discoveries were being made, these dissections, or autopsies, became more common. Autopsies are now regularly performed to discover causes of death. For the same reason, zoos also perform autopsies on animals. These are called necropsies.

Eighteenth-century cartoon of an autopsy of a hanged murderer

Anatomical Art

Despite taboos, people have been looking inside dead people for thousands of years. Not only have they looked inside, but they've drawn what they've seen. Doctors through the ages have learned about the workings of the human body from this art.

Since dinosaurs and trilobites and other prehistoric creatures are extinct, the only way we can learn about them is to study their fossilized remains. **Paleontologists** are fossil specialists, and it's through their work that we know so much about the animals and plants that lived on earth millions of years ago. These two paleontologists (above) are carefully chipping away at the rock that surrounds a rib and vertebrae (back bones) of a mystery sauropod. Sauropods are in the dinosaur family that includes the humongous *Argentinosaurus* and *Diplodocus*.

When human remains are found, forensic scientists are brought in to help answer questions for the legal system. If all that is found is a skeleton, a **forensic anthropologist** will examine the bones to determine the size, age, and sex of the deceased. This information can help identify the victim.

Other Specialties:

- **Forensic entomologist** – examines insects found on or near a body to determine time of death

- **Forensic pathologist** – examines the body and performs an autopsy

- **Forensic toxicologist** – looks for signs of drugs or poisons in the body

- **Forensic odontologist** – examines the teeth and compares them to dental records

- **Forensic botanist** – examines plant matter, including seeds and pollens, found on a dead body

Back From The Dead

From the very beginning people have wanted to do the impossible — bring back, or **resurrect**, the dead.

There have been a multitude of ways that people have tried to bring back their loved ones. They've tried praying and chanting. They've rubbed dead bodies with herbs, or poured wild-mushroom tea down lifeless throats. By the nineteenth century people were trying to shock the dead back to life with electricity. Though these early experiments were failures, they may have provided the inspiration for Mary Shelley to write *Frankenstein*, the story of a monster cobbled together from parts of corpses and brought to life with electricity.

Today, people whose hearts have stopped, who are "dead," are regularly revived. A number of different methods are used to "jump start" the heart — and it turns out that what works best is electricity! Doctors start blood pumping again by sending electric shocks to the heart muscle with "defibrillator" paddles.

Fast response is critical when someone's heart stops beating.

Doctors implant an electrical device in a patient's heart to keep it beating.

Cryonics is the process of freezing and storing the bodies, or sometimes just the heads, of recently deceased people. The hope is that one day they can be brought back to life and cured of whatever illnesses killed them. A major problem with this is that, even with new freezing technology, tissue damage can occur during thawing. So future scientists will not only have to figure how to "reanimate" frozen people, but how to repair cell damage as well.

Can we make clones of extinct animals?

Pick me! Pick me!

To clone an extinct species, we would first have to find undamaged DNA from that animal. Though scientists have been able to map the genetic code of the extinct woolly mammoth (see page 45), so far all the DNA they've found is too damaged to create an actual clone. Cloning a dinosaur presents even more problems. Since dinosaur remains are almost always fossilized, the chances of ever finding usable DNA are extremely slim. But future technologies may solve the problem of reconstruction, so who knows — maybe someday there will be dinosaurs in our backyards!

The first cat was cloned in 2002. Scientists called the kitten Cc, short for carbon copy or copy cat.

What's a Clone?

A clone is a perfect copy of a living thing made from another living thing. Many plants make clones naturally. Identical twins are natural clones. Scientists clone animals artificially by taking a DNA sample, or "genetic fingerprint," from an adult and inserting it into a developing egg. There's already a company that will clone your pet cat...for $50,000!

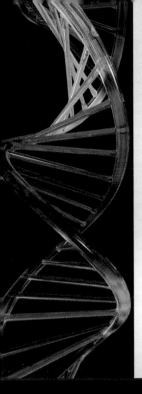

Diagram of the double helix shape of DNA.

I Found a Dead Bird

This book began
with some questions
about a dead bird I found.
So it seems only fitting
to end it with the actual
story of the dead bird.

The dead bird I found was a ruby-throated hummingbird — a male, because its throat glimmered brilliant red. It had flown into a garage on a hot summer day and couldn't find its way out again.

It must have been able to see flowers and trees through a window, and hovered there trying to get out. But it wouldn't have been able to escape through the glass. With nothing to eat, and using all its energy to keep hovering, it would have become weaker and weaker. After only a couple of hours, it would have fallen to the windowsill where it died, for want of food.

The sunny windowsill was very hot and dry. Because hummingbirds are so tiny — barely the size of a big bug — it dried so quickly it didn't have a chance to properly decompose. And that's how I found it, perfectly mummified. And it *did* make me sad, because it's sad when living things die — it's sad, but it's also part of the cycle of life.

Jan Thornhill

Hummingbirds are very high-energy birds. Their wings beat up to 80 times a second, which allows them to hover in one spot or to dart quickly from one flower to another. But all that activity requires an enormous amount of energy, energy hummingbirds get from their main food source — sugary flower nectar. Simply to stay alive, a hummingbird has to drink almost eight times its weight in nectar every day.

Female ruby-throated hummingbirds have pale throats.

Acknowledgments

Without the generosity of numerous people — from scientists to amateur photographers — this book would not have been possible. These generous and thoughtful people include: Joe Pase, Texas Forest Service; Russell Jacobson, Illinois Geographical Survey; Richard Major, Australian Museum; Russ Hopcroft, Institute of Marine Science, University of Alaska; Valerie Behan-Pelletier and Barbara Eamer, Agriculture and Agri-Food Canada; Robert David Siegel, Stanford University; Morgan Vis, Ohio University; and Alex Wild, University of California. I would also like to gratefully acknowledge the financial support of the Ontario Arts Council. And thanks, too, to my family and friends, and particularly to my husband, for putting up with some pretty unorthodox dinner conversation over the past year.

Photo Credits

Index